Giuseppe Gangi

ROME
then and now

ALPA ITALIA EDITRICE
ROMA

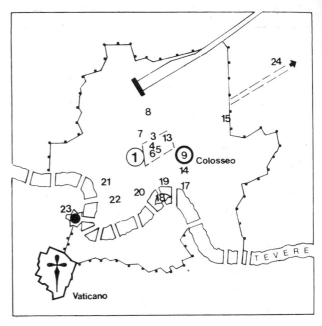

© Copyright 1985 by ALPA ITALIA Editrice srl, Roma
Text by Giuseppe Gangi
Translations by Geoffrey Copleston
Reconstructions: Studio AEP, Arch. Carlo Boldreghini, Rome
Lay-out: Arch. Glauco Cartocci
Basic photographic material:
Roxyfilm, C. Tonini, Rome;
Scala, Florence, n. 1,2;
Publiaerfoto, Milan, n. 9, 22, 24;
Fotocielo, Rome, n. 15, 18, 21, 23.
Photolitography: Gamba srl, Rome.

Index

A brief outline of the urban development of ancient Rome

The aim of this book is to give the hurried tourist an idea of what the «Urbs» looked like at the height of its splendour.

The Palatine, one of the Seven Hills of Rome and an ideal place for an urban settlement, was, in fact, occupied by a group of shepherds who controlled, from that strategic point, the ford across the River Tiber along which there was commercial traffic.

According to legend, the city was founded by Romulus in 753 B.C. His successors enlarged the settlement to cover the other hills as they gradually extended their authority and dominion over the neighbouring tribes (Sabines and Latins).

The city and its lands were ruled by a king in the early days but the monarchy came to a sudden end with the fall of the seventh king: Tarquin the Superb.

A republic was founded in 509 B.C. and its ordinances were enforced by various magistrates: Consuls, Praetors, Aediles, Censors and Tribunes of the Plebs.

During the Republican period many great public buildings, such as the Curia, the Temple of Saturn, that of the Dioscuri (Castor and Pollux) and the Temple of Concordia on the slopes of the Capitol, were built. In 390 B.C. Rome passed through one of the most dramatic periods of her history when she was invaded, occupied and sacked by a horde of predatory Gauls.

It was their leader, Brennus, who, as he demanded a huge ransom for the city, uttered the famous phrase «Vae victis!» - «Woe to the conquered!».

The Roman General, Furius Camillus, persuaded the Romans not to move to Veii (now Veio), as they intended, but to set to work and rebuild the city as quickly as possible.

A few years later, in 378 B.C., a strong belt of walls, called the Servian Walls, were built of volcanic «tufo». These walls had a perimeter of nearly seven miles and they enclosed all the legendary Seven Hills of Rome (Aventine, Palatine, Caelian, Esquiline, Capitoline, Viminal and Quirinal).

During the centuries which followed, after waging terrible wars against the Etruscans and the Samnites, Rome succeeded in establishing a firm hold on almost all the Italian peninsula. Also during this period, however, thanks to the efforts of the Censor Appius Claudius Caecus (312 B.C.), two great civil works were built. One was the first of the great Roman roads, a great artery that linked central Italy with the south: the Appian Way (now the Via Appia Antica), the second was the first great completely undergound aqueduct to bring water to Rome. Nearly a century later, in 291 B.C. a temple to Aesculapius, the god of healing, was founded on the Tiber Island.

In 264 B.C. Rome engaged in a mortal struggle with the mighty commercial city-state of Carthage. Carthage was a maritime power and mistress of the Mediterranean. The three Punic wars that followed were long and hard fought but, after a long series of victories and defeats, Rome triumphed over her stubborn rival in 202 B.C. at the battle of Zama in what is now Tunisia. Nearly a century and a half later, Rome finally put an end to Carthage by conquering and destroying the city in 146 B.C.

In this long period of time the construction of many important monuments and buildings, such as the Circus Flaminius (221 B.C.) and the Porcia, Aemilia and Sempronia basilicas in the Roman Forum (184 B.C.), was carried out.

The ancient Roman basilicas were great halls used for the administration of justice and the transaction of public and private business. In addition, the Forum Boarium and the Forum Holitorium, stores for grain and other staple foods, as well as other buildings, were erected. In 144 B.C., a new aqueduct brought the Aqua Marcia to Rome. Then, in 126 B.C., yet another brought the Aqua Tepula.

The first stone bridges spanned the Tiber. In 179-142 B.C. further arches were added to the Pons Aemilius; the Pons Mulvus (the Milvian Bridge), built in 207 B.C. was entirely rebuilt in 109 B.C. and is still in use today.

The victory over Carthage had made Rome powerful at sea, as well as powerful on land, and mistress of the Mediteranean at last. This dominion brought supremacy in the east, with the conquest of the kingdoms that were part of Alexander the Great's empire.

Contact with the culture of the Orient opened the eyes of the Roman world to new knowledge and new ideas in many fields, including that of architecture.

The use of the arch transformed the square-cut concept of the trabeated monuments in the Greek style into a concept of curves. This, and the use of the vault, gave a new expression to Roman architecture which was now embellished with rare, oriental marbles. The city grew and the old houses in dull but solid «tufo» or wood were replaced by many-storied brick buildings, palaces and temples faced with marble and the narrow winding streets by broad thoroughfares.

This great flux of construction had its greatest inspiration and vigour in the Age of Silla (82 B.C.). To this period belongs the building of the celebrated Tabularium which housed the archives of the Roman state. It is a work by Quintius Lutatius Catulus (78 B.C.).

With Julius Caesar (101-44 B.C.), Rome's conquests increased until they formed a vast empire that covered the major part of the ancient world. But Caesar's appointment as Dictator marked the end of an epoch, of a glorious age, and the beginning of the Imperial Age for Ancient Rome.

With the «Lex de Urbe Augenda», Julius Caesar introduced a new town planning scheme for a vast transformation of the city. It involved the deviation of the course of the Tiber towards the Vatican Hills, thus enlarging the Campus Martius up to the «Orti di Trastevere».

Moreover, since the Roman Forum had become too small to cater for the multiple and complex needs of a city whose population at that time numbered about one million, Julius Caesar ordered the building of a new Forum, dominated in the central part by a temple dedicated to Venus Genetrix.

However, Caesar's death interrupted the town planning scheme and progress was halted until the city underwent a renovation under Augustus (23 B.C.-14 A.D.) who divided it into 14 regions, with seven Fire Brigades and Police Forces. He also raised a temple dedicated to the memory of Julius Caesar.

Augustus, too, built a new Forum with a temple dedicated to Mars Ultor in the centre, but his most important work was the draining of the unhealthy Campus Martius, which he chose as a site for his Mausoleum, the Ara Pacis, and for the Solarium. Agrippa, son-in-law to Augustus, who began the building of the Pantheon, built the first public bathing establishment with a park and ornamental lakes (Thermae Agrippae), which brought still more water to Rome through aqueducts among which were the Aqua Julia, in 33 B.C. and the Aqua Virgo in 19 B.C. In 2 B.C. Augustus brought the Aqua Alsietina to Rome to supply the «Naumachiae» or arenas for naval battles in Trastevere.

In 64 A.D., under Nero, a great fire broke out in Rome and reduced a large part of the city to ashes. After this disaster the emperor brought into effect a plan for the reconstruction of the city. It called for robust buildings in brick or stone with interior courtyards and above all the important innovation of porticoes along the streets to protect the fronts of the «insulae» or apartment houses from future fires. In spite of this plan the real reconstruction of the city was carried out principally by the emperors of the «gens Flavia», the Flavian clan: Vespasian (69-79 A.D.), Titus (79-81 A.D.) and Domitian (81-96 A.D.). To Vespasian and Titus we owe the building of the Flavian Amphitheatre, better known as the Colosseum.

To Domitian are attributed numerous works which completely changed the face of the city, such as Domitian's Circus or Circus Agonalis (today Piazza Navona) in the Campus Martius, the Odeon (a theatre) close by the Circus, and a new artificial lake for «Naumachiae» or sea-fights on the banks of the Tiber, the re-building of the Domus Tiberiana on the Palatine Hill and the building, «ex novo», of a magnificent Imperial Palace, Domus Augustana, and on the Velia (a narrow ridge connecting the Palatine and the Oppian Hills) the building of a triumphal arch dedicated to his brother, Titus.

After the emperors of the «gens Flavia», came the brief reign of the elderly Nerva, who was followed by Trajan (98-117 A.D.). With the help of the architect Apollodorus of Damascus, a Greek, this emperor built the great Forum which bears his name, together with its markets, shops, libraries and the towering column with marvellous reliefs covering the whole shaft.

The next emperor, Hadrian (who built the wall between Scotland and England), reigned from 117 A.D. to 138 A.D.. He enriched Rome with the building of his huge Mausoleum (today Castel Sant'Angelo) and the Temple of Venus and Rome (close to the Colosseum), designed by Apollodorus of Damascus and once the largest in Ancient Rome. To Hadrian, we also owe the complete rebuilding of the Pantheon.

The last period of the Rome of the Caesars can boast of two emperors of great stature: Diocletian (284-305 A.D.) and Constantine the Great (306-337 A.D.). To the first is due the constitutional reform of the empire and the introduction of the Tetrarchy (an attempt to provide each part of the empire with a ruler and to establish and order non-hereditary succession). He also embellished the city with his Baths, the largest in Rome, capable of serving 3,600 bathers. Today the ruins of these thermal baths house the National Museum of Archaeology and the Church of Santa Maria degli Angeli. This wonderful adaption and restoration in the field of the conversion of a «Thermae» is due to the genius of Michaelangelo.

After his victory over Maxentius in 312 A.D., at a place called «Saxa Rubra», just outside Rome on the Via Flaminia, Constantine had another public bathing establishment built on the Quirinal Hill and finished the building of the Basilica of Maxentius.

The Arch of Constantine, in front of the Colosseum which we admire today, was raised in his honour by the Senate to give thanks for his exceptional merits as an emperor and «Defensor Civitatis».

This was the end of the pagan world. Although a follower of Mithraism, Constantine adopted Christianity which soon became the «de facto» religion of the empire. One by one the old temples were closed down and they, and other remarkable monuments, were abandoned. With the removal of the capital of the empire to Byzantium (Constantinople), Rome lost the rank of universal «Urbs» thus beginning the sad period of decline, depopulation and decadence, while the Christian faith was triumphantly propagated.

1.
Roman Forum *(total)*

It was born and took its place as the political, religious, legal and administrative centre of the ancient city after the valley, which lies between the Palatine, Capitol and Quirinal Hills, was drained by the famous Cloaca Maxima. It became the Forum, that is to say «The Square». The ruined state of the Forum today is due to the demolition carried out by man rather than to the destructive action of time.

1. The Arch of Septimius Severus.
It is low down on the left of the picture and was built in the year 203 A.D.

2. The Curia.

This was the ancient seat of the Senate of Rome, according to tradition founded by the third king of Rome, Tullus Hostilius in the seventh century before Christ. It has been destroyed and rebuilt many times and the present building goes back to the last reconstruction by Diocletian at the end of the third century A.D. In front of the Curia is preserved the area of the Comitium, where meetings of the populace took place, the earliest political activity of the united city.

3. The Basilica Aemilia

Built in 179 B.C. by the Censors Marcus Aemilius Lepidus and Marcus Fulvius Nobilior it was destroyed and the remains one can see were left after the last destruction by Alaric the Visigoth in 410 A.D.
As they had wide, covered colonnades, the basilicas were used, in bad weather, for all the activities that were usually carried on in the open, such as the administration of justice, business and the exchange of goods and money.

4. Temple of Antoninus and Faustina (141 A.D.).

5. Forum of Nerva or Transitory Forum (97 A.D.).

So called because, by crossing its long, narrow square, one reached the adjacent Fora.

6. Basilica of Maxentius (306 A.D.).

Begun by Maxentius and finished by Constantine, like all Roman Basilicas it was used for business deals and the administration of justice.

7. Temple of Venus and Rome (135 A.D.).

8. Coloseum (80 A.D.).

9. The House of the Vestals

In its present aspect it corresponds to the last restoration by Septimius Severus after the fire of 191 A.D.

10. The Palatine Hill.

With the imposing ruins of the Palace of the Caesars.

11. The Temple of Vesta (early 7th. cent. B.C., last reconstruction by Giulia Domna, end of 2nd. cent. A.D.)

12. The Temple of Divus Julius (29 B.C.).

13. The Temple of the Dioscuri «Castor and Pollux» (5th cent. B.C.).

14. Basilica Julia.

Julius Caesar had it built in the year 54 B.C. The last reconstruction bears the date 377 A.D. The hall or court room measured about 160 feet by 333 feet.

15. Temple of Saturn (498 B.C.).

16. The Rostra (Original building 338 B.C. extant ruins 29 B.C.).

It was the stage for the orators who spoke in the Roman Forum, about eighty feet long by forty feet wide.

2.
The Roman Forum *(seen from the Arch of Titus)*

1. The Basilica Julia (54 B.C.).

2. The Temple of Saturn.

The temple was erected in 498 B.C.; the State treasure was kept in its cellar. On December 17th., the anniversary of the dedication of the temple, the celebrations for the end of the year, called Saturnalia, took place. They were of an orgiastic character.

3. The Temple of Vespasian.

Built in 81 A.D. by Domitian in honour of his father, Vespasian, and his brother, Titus, it was later restored by the emperors Septimus Severus and Caracalla.

4. The Temple of Concordia.

Built in the year 367 B.C. by Marcus Furius Camillus to commemorate the agreement reached between the Patricians and the Plebs that confirmed the political equality of the two classes. This temple was also used as a museum.

5. The Arch of Septimius Severus (203 A.D.).

It was erected, as stated in the inscription on both sides of the upper section, by the Senate and People of Rome in honour of the emperor Lucius Septimius Severus and his two sons Caracalla and Geta, whose name was erased after he had been killed by his brother.

The four great panels above the two lateral arches illustrate episodes in the victorious Parthian wars conducted by Severus.

Panels of military undertaking in imitation of those on the columns of Trajan and Marcus Aurelius follow one another in chronological order and the unusual way in which the planes overlap give us the idea of triumphal painting carried out on large cartoons that were carried in the processions in honour of the emperor.

6. The Tabularium (78 B.C.).

This was the State Archives of Rome and, standing close against the Capitoline Hill, it forms a back-ground for the Valley of the **Roman** Forum. Later it was used as a store for salt and as a prison. Today it is City Hall. **The** upper part of the building belongs to the Senatorial Palace and is a 16th Century reconstruction.

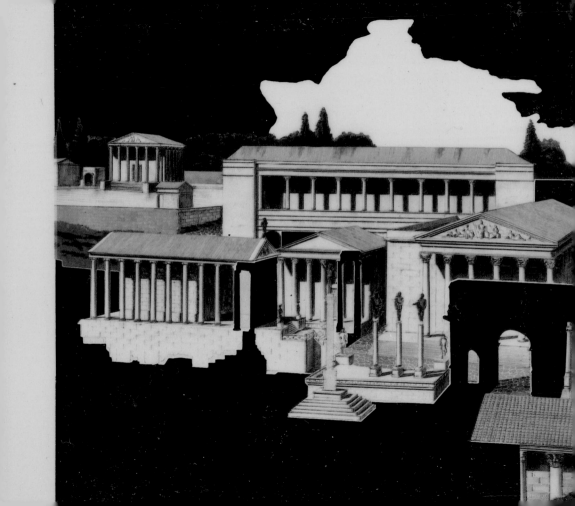

3.
The Temple of Antoninus and Faustina *(141 A.D.)*

The erection of this temple was decreed by the Roman Senate to commemorate the deification of Faustina, wife of Antoninus Pius.

Upon the emperor's death the temple was dedicated also to him. In the early Middle Ages (12th. Cent.) it became a church, dedicated to «San Lorenzo in Miranda».

The oblique grooves at the top of the columns were to stop the ropes from slipping when attempts were made to pull down this ancient monument.

This is just one of the examples of vandalism and pillage of ancient monuments carried out during the Middle Ages.

3.
The Temple of Antoninus and Faustina *(141 A.D.)*

The erection of this temple was decreed by the Roman Senate to commemorate the deification of Faustina, wife of Antoninus Pius.

Upon the emperor's death the temple was dedicated also to him. In the early Middle Ages (12th. Cent.) it became a church, dedicated to «San Lorenzo in Miranda».

The oblique grooves at the top of the columns were to stop the ropes from slipping when attempts were made to pull down this ancient monument.

This is just one of the examples of vandalism and pillage of ancient monuments carried out during the Middle Ages.

4.
The Temple of Julius Caesar *(29 B.C.)*

This temple was built by Augustus in honour of his deified great-uncle and adoptive father, Julius Caesar.

In the hollowed out space of the podium there remains the nucleus of the circular altar raised almost exactly on the spot on which the body of the great general and statesman was cremated.

It was close to this altar that Mark Anthony delivered his famous burial speech: «Friends! Romans! Countrymen! Lend me your ears! I come to bury Caesar, not to praise him. The evil that men do lives after them, the good is oft interrèd with their bones».

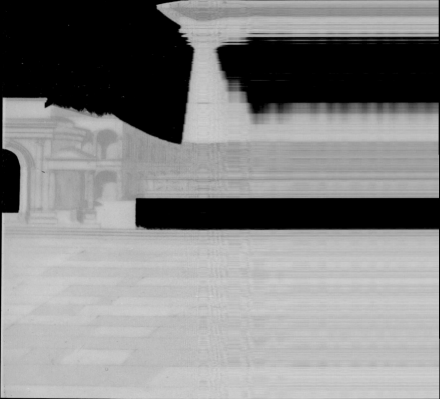

24.
The tomb of Caecilia Metella *(1st. Cent. B.C.)*
The Via Appia Antica *(312 B.C.)*

The Via Appia Antica, begun in 312 B.C. by the Consul Appius Claudius Caecus, after whom it is named, was the first of the great consular roads. It linked Rome with the south of Italy, reaching after an extra leg had been added in 190 B.C., to the port of Brindisi 'from whence one sailed for Greece, Asia Minor and Egypt. It was a Roman custom to line the sides of the consulare roads with monumental tombs to impress visitors to the «Urbs». One of the best preserved tombs is that built for Caecilia Metella daughter of Quintus Caecilius Metellus Creticus and wife to Marcus Licinius Crassus, one of Julius Caesar's generals in the Gallic Wars.

The drum of the tomb has a diameter of 66 feet and rests on a square base of concrete whose marble facing has been removed.

In the 13th Cent. it became a tower in the walls of the Caetani Castle.

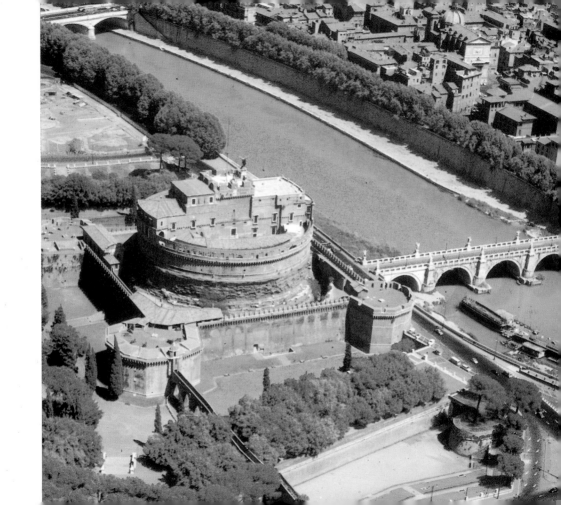

23.
Hadrian's Tomb

The emperor wished to build, for himself and his family, an imposing funeral monument. The construction of the mausoleum was begun in 130 A.D. and finished a year after the emperor's death in 139 A.D. by Antoninus Pius. It is now known as Castel Sant'Angelo.

The Ponte Sant'Angelo, adorned with statues by Bernini, is the ancient Pons Helios (134 A.D.), built to give access to the mausoleum. During the Middle Ages many buildings of ancient Rome were converted to other uses. The most striking example is the mighty fortress which was built on the base of Hadrian's Tomb.

22.
Stadium of Domitian *(86 A.D.)*

With a capacity for 30,000 spectators, it was built for athletic «Games» in the Greek tradition (as opposed to gladiatorial «Games»). The Stadium was also occasionally used for gladiatorial games and «venationes» or wild beast hunts and combats of beast against beast.

Piazza Navona, built on the ruins of the stadium, retains the shape of the track in its plan and dimensions. The present appearance of the Piazza is due to the architects Bernini (1598-1680) and Borromini (1599-1667) working for Pope Innocent Xth Pamphili (1644-55) who wished to make it the centre of Baroque Rome.

The fantastic architectural whole, orchestrated by Bernini, has its most expressive element in the Fountain of the Four Rivers (1651) in the centre of the square. It is surmounted by an Egyptian obelisk.

Borromini is responsible for the church of St. Agnes in Agone (1657) which we see on the left of the picture.

21.
Pantheon

The original building whose remains were found under the «pronaos», dates back to 27 B.C., was the work of Agrippa. The present building goes back to the times of Hadrian and was built between 118 and 125 A.D. This temple was dedicated to all the gods (in greek Pantheos).

The temple is a rotunda with an internal diameter of 143 feet, equal to the distance from the floor to the top of the dome. The dome is an exceptional feat of engineering being made of a single pouring of concrete over a wooden frame. It is a perfect hemisphere and rests on the cylinder formed by the 20 ft. thick walls of brick-faced concrete. Inside the temple the wall itself is converted by semi-circular chambers into eight piers which are the most highly compressed parts of the building.

The skylight at the top of the dome (30 feet in diameter) is the only source of light in the building; and the rain which comes through it is drained away by the holes in the centre of the floor.

In the Pantheon, (a Christian church since the 7th cent. A.D.), are buried the kings of Italy and the painter Raphael who died in April 1520 at the early age of 37.

21.
Pantheon

The original building whose remains were found under the «pronaos», dates back to 27 B.C., was the work of Agrippa. The present building goes back to the times of Hadrian and was built between 118 and 125 A.D. This temple was dedicated to all the gods (in greek Pantheos).

The temple is a rotunda with an internal diameter of 143 feet, equal to the distance from the floor to the top of the dome. The dome is an exceptional feat of engineering being made of a single pouring of concrete over a wooden frame. It is a perfect hemisphere and rests on the cylinder formed by the 20 ft. thick walls of brick-faced concrete. Inside the temple the wall itself is converted by semi-circular chambers into eight piers which are the most highly compressed parts of the building.

The skylight at the top of the dome (30 feet in diameter) is the only source of light in the building; and the rain which comes through it is drained away by the holes in the centre of the floor.

In the Pantheon, (a Christian church since the 7th cent. A.D.), are buried the kings of Italy and the painter Raphael who died in April 1520 at the early age of 37.

20.
Four temples of the Republican Era

In the picture we see four temples built during the period from the 4th Cent. to the 2nd Cent. B.C., in the Republican Era of Rome's history. In ancient times these temples formed the sacred area of the Campus Martius.

Not far from them is the Curia and Theatre of Pompey, where Julius Caesar was assassinated on the Ides of March 44 B.C. The last words attributed to him are: «**Tu quoque, Brute, fili mi!**» («You too, Brutus, my son!»).

Immediately to the right we can see the temple designated «Temple A» which dates back to the 3rd Cent. B.C.. It has undergone many radical transformations, the last being in Imperial times.

In the centre of the photograph we see a round building, Temple «B», founded by Quintius Lutatius Catulus in 102 B.C. to commemorate the victory over the Cimbri (a Germanic tribe). Then there is Temple «C», perhaps of the 4th Cent B.C., and probably the oldest of the four. Last, we have Temple «D» partially covered by the street, Via Florida. This temple dates back to the 2nd Cent. B.C., but the remains are what is left of a late Republican reconstruction.

19.
The Temple of the Sosian Apollo and the Temple of Bellona

The temple of Apollo Medice, in the centre of the picture, was first built in 431 B.C., and rebuilt in its present form in 34 B.C., by the Consul Gaius Sosius, hence the appellative «Sosian».

Here Apollo was worshipped for his powers of healing. The «Cella» was decorated with statues and pictures and was frequently used as a meeting place for the Senate.

On the right is the Temple of Bellona, the Roman godess of War. This temple was built by Appius Claudius Caecus in 296 B.C.
On the left you can see a part of the Theatre of Marcellus (11 B.C.).

18.
The Tiber Island

The island still preserves the shape of a ship which was given it in ancient Roman times.

In the centre of the island stood the temple dedicated to Aesculapius, the god of healing.

The area where the temple stood is now occupied by the medieval church of St. Bartholemew. The island is connected to the banks of the Tiber by two bridges, both dating back to ancient Roman times.

Low down on the left one can see an arch of the Pons Aemilius (179-142 B.C.), the first masonry bridge to be built in Rome.

On the right is the Pons Fabricius, built in 62 B.C., one of the most ancient in Rome that has been handed down to us almost intact. On the left is the Pons Cestius, built in 46 B.C., but entirely rebuilt in 368 A.D.

On the opposite side facing the church is the hospital of Fatebenefratelli, founded in 1548, which carries on the island's tradition of caring for both body and soul.

17.

The temples known as the «Temple of Vesta» *(end of 2nd Cent. B.C.)* and the «Temple of Fortune» *(early 2nd. Cent B.C.)*

The round temple was dedicated to **Hercules Holivarius**, divine patron of the oil merchants, the most ancient example of a marble temple in Rome.

The other square temple was dedicated to **Portunus**, the divinity that protected the nearby river port. It is one of the best preserved ancient buildings in Rome. Perfect in its form and in its lines; it is a rare example of greco-italic architecture.

16.
Baths of Caracalla *(interior)*

A glimpse of Roman life in the Baths: in the foreground is one of the two vestibules that lead to the «*Natatio*», that is to say the open-air, cold water swimming pool.

15.
The Baths of Caracalla seen from above

The building of the baths or «Thermae» was started by Caracalla in 212 A.D. and completed around 216 A.D. The outer perimeter walls were added by Heliogabalus and Alexander Severus.

The bathing establishments consisted of various buildings for public and private baths, swimming, massage, exercise, gymnastics, and so on.

There were also libraries, gardens and conference rooms.
The establishment was huge and could accomodate 1,600 bathers.
The dimensions of the outside perimeter were 1,320 feet by 1,082 feet.

14.
The Circus Maximus

This enormous structure, located between the Palatine and Aventine hills, was used principally for chariot races. It is said that the circus could hold 250,000 spectators, an enormous number even for modern times.

According to tradition it was founded by Tarquinius Priscus. The stands for the spectators, originally in wood, were later rebuilt in brickwork.
In the year 329 B.C., the «Carceres» or curved starting gate on the north side were built; but a permanent masonry structure was not built until the beginning of the 2nd Cent. A.D. There were various reconstructions and enlargements in Imperial times.

The huge building measured 1,980 feet in length and 660 feet in width. In the centre of the track there was a «backbone» (Spina); and the chariots made seven circuits of this in a single race. Two great obelisks were placed in the centre of the spina. The great king Totila the Ostrogoth, was the last king to offer chariot races to the Romans in the year 549 A.D.

The charioteers competed for the colours of the four factions: White, Green, Blue and Red. The chariot races aroused an enormous enthusiasm in the Romans, in fact, bloody brawls between rival supporters were frequent.

On the left, above the Circus rises the splendid, imposing mass of the Palace of the Caesars.

13.
The Temple of Venus and Rome *(135 A.D.)*

Apollodorus of Damascus designed this temple to the emperor Hadrian's specifications: two cells with apses, back to back. The cell dedicated to the Dea Roma opening towards the Forum and that dedicated to Venus opening towards the Colosseum. Like all the ancient monuments in Rome, it was stripped of its marble facing in the Middle Ages. Moreover, the gilded bronze roofing tiles were used by Pope Honorius I (625-638 A.D.) to re-cover the basilican church of St. Peter in the Vatican, which was demolished by Pope Julius II (1503-1513) to make way for the present church. The temple was used as a marble quarry right up until the 15th Century.

This was the largest temple in ancient Rome (480ft. × 330ft.), and was surrounded by a portico with 150 columns.

12.
Roman public latrine

The public toilets in the Colosseum were probably like this latrine photographed at Ostia Antica.

We can see that they were for collective use and built with remarkably modern techniques and hygienic measures.

11.
Colosseum, gladiatorial combats

The gladiators, recruited from condemned criminals, slaves, Roman citizens and freedmen, were trained in special schools and divided into various categories with various types of arms, armour and combat according to physique or race.

Here we see, on the left, a picture of a «Retiarius» fighting a «Myrmillo».

The «retiarius», on the left, is equipped with a bell-shaped fishing net in which he attempts to entangle his opponent and then kill him with his trident. The equipment of the «myrmillo», the gladiator on the right, is so-called because of the fish on his helmet (sea fish in Greek = mormylos) and it gives us an idea of the richness and fantasy of the uniforms of those legendary fighters.

The fallen gladiators asked for mercy from the emperor, (or whoever else was providing the games), and he having consulted the crowd, gave his verdict:... thumbs up- life..., thumbs down- death!

Here we see the victor carrying out the sentence. As the gladiators entered the arena they greeted the emperor: «**Ave, Caesar! Morituri te salutant**!» ...Hail, Caesar! Greetings from men about to die!

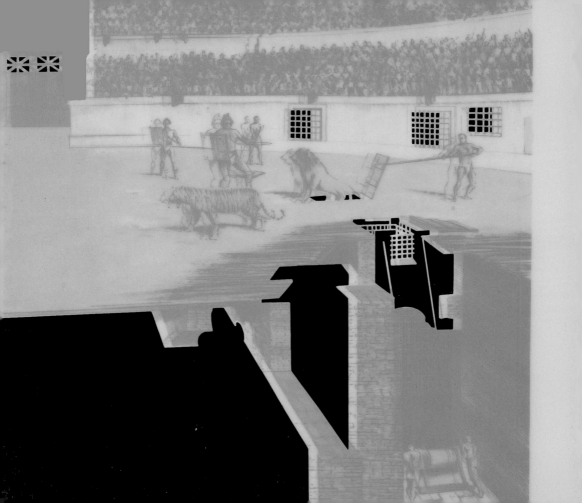

10.
The Arena of the Colosseum

The games in the amphitheatre consisted of:
gladiatorial combats (fights between men); **venationes** (men against wild beast); and perhaps even **naumachiae** (naval battles). The supports of the arena were in wood and could be removed to permit the oval to be flooded.

This sequence shows the reconstruction of the arena and the methods used to bring the wild beasts up to it.

The animals were prodded out of their cages with goads and made to enter primitive counterpoise lifts.

9.
The Colosseum, seen from above

The great amphitheatre was built by the emperor Vespasian (Titus Flavius Vespasianus) to immortalize the name of the Flavian clan (gens Flavia). It was inaugurated by the emperor Titus in the year 80 A.D. It took eight years to build and rises to a height of 165 feet. The plan is an ellipse whose axes are 610 feet by 515 feet. The «stalls», consisting of steps rising from the oval of the arena to the balcony, could seat about 50,000 spectators.

The external architecture consists of three orders or storeys of arches (80 arches per storey) topped by an attic of solid masonry decorated with Corinthian pilasters. Between the arches on the ground floor there are attached three-quarter columns of quasi-Doric order, on the first floor there is the Ionic order and on the second floor, the Corinthian order. The Arena of the Colosseum was a vast oval space floored with wood which has naturally, disappeared, but the supporting walls for the flooring can still be seen, as can the corridors underneath the arena. These corridors and rooms housed the services necessary for the games: lifts, animal cages, stage apparatus and so on.

Note the velarium, an immense awning which, on special occasions, was stretched with a daring manoeuvre carried out by a special squad of sailors from the Imperial Fleet at Misenum, over the amphitheatre to protect the spectators from the sun.

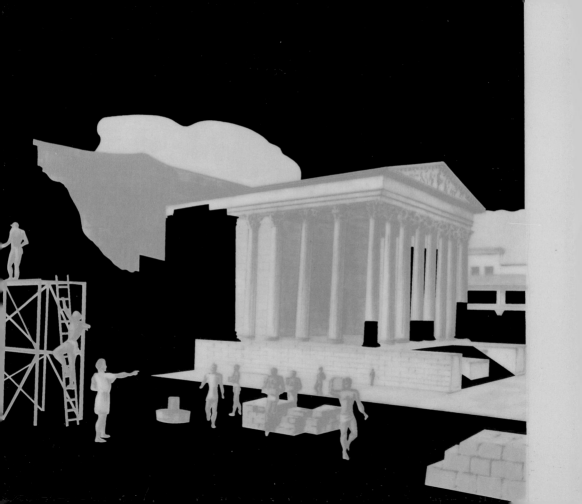

8.
The Forum of Augustus *(2 B.C.)*

With this Forum Augustus intended to enlarge the area of the Roman Forum and the Forum of Caesar (Forum Julium), which had become overcrowded. Augustus created new space for the multitudinous peoples of every race and colour of the Roman world who came to the living, throbbing heart of the empire.

Built to commemorate the victory in 42 B.C. at Philippi in Macedonia over Brutus and Cassius, conspirators in the plot to assassinate Julius Caesar, it was completed and inaugurated 40 years later in 2 B.C.

7.
The Forum of Caesar *(54 B.C.)*

After five hundred years the Roman Forum had become insufficient for the political requirements of Rome. Julius Caesar, therefore, decided to enlarge the political centre of the city by building a new monumental Forum (54 A.D.) and requisitioned valuable land on the slopes of the Capitoline Hill. He levelled the area and built a Forum sufficient to the needs of those days.

The work was begun by Julius Caesar in 54 B.C. and finished, after his death by assassination, by his successor Octavian Augustus.

In the centre of the photograph one can see the three columns belonging to the Temple of Venus Genetrix, built as a grateful offering to the goddess for her guidance in the victorious battle of Pharsalus in which Julius Caesar beat Pompey (48 B.C.), but entirely rebuilt under Domitian and inaugurated by Trajan in 113 A.D.

6.
The Temple of Castor and Pollux *(484 B.C.)*

This temple was built by the dictator Aulus Postumius Albino to respect a vow made during the battle of Lake Regillus in 499 B.C. and dedicated by his son in 484 B.C. According to legend, in this battle, the Heavenly Twins, Castor and Pollux, guided the Romans to victory over the Tarquins and Latins. Immediately after the battle, having brought news of the victory to Rome, the Twins were seen watering their horses at the spring of Lacus Juturnae close to the Temple of Vesta.

The three columns, among the most elegant of classical antiquity, belong to the last reconstruction in the time of Augustus (6th. Cent. A.D.).

The Arch of Augustus *(29-19 B.C.)*

This arch was built to commemorate the victory of Actium (September 31 B.C.).

In the year 19 B.C. after the recovery of the standards from the Parthians, two lateral arches were added.

On the inside panel of these fornices the lists of magistrates (Fasti Consulares) and records of triumphs (Fasti Triumphales) were exposed.

5.
The Temple of Vesta *(7th. Cent. B.C.)*

Founded in the times of the Seven Kings, it had a circular plan that reproduced the shape of the ancient hut.

In this temple the Vestal Virgins kept the Sacred Fire, symbol of the life of the Urbs. The six priestesses, chosen from the most noble families of Rome, were obliged to remain chaste for thirty years. The vow of chastity was absolute and if one of them broke it, she was condemned to be buried alive.

The temple was the last reconstructed after the fire of 191 A.D. by Julia Domna, second wife of Septimius Severus.

4.
The Temple of Julius Caesar *(29 B.C.)*

This temple was built by Augustus in honour of his deified great-uncle and adoptive father, Julius Caesar.

In the hollowed out space of the podium there remains the nucleus of the circular altar raised almost exactly on the spot on which the body of the great general and statesman was cremated.

It was close to this altar that Mark Anthony delivered his famous burial speech: «Friends! Romans! Countrymen! Lend me your ears! I come to bury Caesar, not to praise him. The evil that men do lives after them, the good is oft interrèd with their bones».